ESSENTIAL LIBRARY OF SOCIAL CHANGE

ANIMAL RIGHTS MOVEMENT

ABDO
Publishing Company

NO to
Grimston
Beagle
Farm

PeTA

ESSENTIAL LIBRARY OF SOCIAL CHANGE

ANIMAL RIGHTS MOVEMENT

by Laura Perdew

Content Consultant

Dr. Joseph L. Gaziano
Political Science Department, Lewis University

CREDITS

Published by ABDO Publishing Company, PO Box 398166, Minneapolis, MN 55439. Copyright © 2014 by Abdo Consulting Group, Inc. International copyrights reserved in all countries. No part of this book may be reproduced in any form without written permission from the publisher. The Essential Library™ is a trademark and logo of ABDO Publishing Company.

Printed in the United States of America,
North Mankato, Minnesota
062013
092013

♻ THIS BOOK CONTAINS AT LEAST 10% RECYCLED MATERIALS.

Editor: Angela Wiechmann
Series Designer: Emily Love

Photo credits: Benjamin Wright/PA Wire/AP Images, cover, 2; iStockphoto/Thinkstock, 6, 69, 85, 97; Bettmann/Corbis/AP Images, 10, 56; Albert L. Ortega/Getty Images, 17; Joseph Bryon/Library of Congress, 18; Hulton Archive/Getty Images, 21; Library of Congress, 23, 26; National Railway Museum/SSPL/Getty Images, 29; Harris & Ewing/Library of Congress, 30; H. F. Davis/Topical Press Agency/Getty Images, 35; AP Images, 37; Gamma-Keystone/Getty Images, 39; Steve Pyke/Getty Images, 40; Carol M. Highsmith/Library of Congress, 44; Sue McDonald/Shutterstock Images, 46; Siqui Sanchez/Getty Images, 50; Tim Clary/AP Images, 52; Gerard Koudenburg/Shutterstock Images, 59; Tao-Chuan Yeh/AFP/Getty Images, 63; Shayna Brennan/AP Images, 64; Digital Frog International/AP Images, 71; Libor Zavoral/CTK/AP Images, 72; The Humane Society of the United States/AP Images, 77; Steve Yeater/AP Images, 81; Rafa Rivas/AFP/Getty Images, 86; Yogen Shah/India Today Group/Getty Images, 90; Oli Scarff/Getty Images, 94; Red Line Editorial, 100, 101

Library of Congress Control Number: 2013932964

Cataloging-in-Publication Data

Perdew, Laura.
 Animal rights movement / Laura Perdew.
   p. cm. -- (Essential library of social change)
Includes bibliographical references and index.
ISBN 978-1-61783-884-2
1. Animal rights--Juvenile literature. 2. Animal welfare--Juvenile literature. I. Title.
179/.3--dc23

2013932964

CONTENTS

CHAPTER 1

SILVER SPRING MONKEYS

In the early 1980s, Edward Taub was the lead research scientist at the Institute for Behavioral Research (IBR) in Silver Spring, Maryland. He had a large facility and more than $100,000 a year in federal funding from the National Institutes of Health (NIH).[1] The NIH is a large medical research agency under the US Department of Health and Human Services. With macaque monkeys as his test subjects, Taub studied the rehabilitation of impaired or disabled limbs. Taub believed his work would someday help treat stroke and accident victims.

Around the same time, activists Alex Pacheco and Ingrid Newkirk cofounded an animal rights organization called People for the Ethical Treatment of Animals (PETA) in Norfolk, Virginia. In 1980, they had fewer than 20 members.[2] Nonetheless, they knew their small grassroots organization could expose the abuse of animals used for food production and experimentation. Newkirk had already reformed the city dog pound in Washington, DC. And together, they had picketed

ANIMALS USED FOR EXPERIMENTATION

One of the greatest concerns for animal rights activists is the use of animals in research laboratories such as Taub's. To this day, animals are used for testing cosmetics and household products, for dissection in classrooms, as teaching aids, in military research, for psychological studies, and in many other categories of scientific research. It is estimated tens of millions of animals are used yearly in such research.

Because laboratories are mostly unregulated, little attention has been given to the conditions and procedures these animals endure. Such practices are sanctioned as normal procedure in the scientific community. Many are funded by government grants. In the years since the Silver Spring monkeys case, the animal rights movement has worked to expose these practices and eliminate the use of animals for research.

slaughterhouses and protested government agencies overseeing animal agriculture and research.

Their next focus was to reveal what went on behind the closed doors of federally funded animal research facilities. The pair knew PETA members could not simply walk into a lab to see the conditions under which laboratory animals were kept. Pacheco decided to go undercover. He selected IBR from a list of animal research facilities registered with the US Department of Agriculture (USDA).

Pacheco applied for a job as a research assistant at IBR in May 1981. He had no prior experience. Taub believed Pacheco was simply interested in scientific research and offered him the position without pay. When Pacheco began the undercover mission, he did not know what he was getting himself into. From his first steps into the lab, Pacheco was horrified by the conditions. The smell was overpowering. The monkeys' cages were small—only 17.5 inches wide by 36 inches deep (44.5 cm by 91.5 cm).[3] They were old, rusty, and caked with fecal matter. Medical records littered the surgery room. Rat droppings dotted every surface. Dirty, discarded clothes were tossed haphazardly about. And Pacheco saw cockroaches, both dead and alive, in the sink, in drawers, and on the floor. Taub and the others working in the lab seemed unfazed by the conditions.

VOICES OF THE MOVEMENT

In an interview, Pacheco described the determination it took to work undercover in the Silver Spring monkeys case:

66 **When I got home [from the laboratory] I would have to strip, stand under the shower and scrub to get the smell out of my skin and hair. I could see the evidence of IBR's filth and decomposition under my nails and in the lines of my skin. If only I could have scrubbed the image of the monkeys out of my mind. It became increasingly difficult to go back to IBR every day, yet I knew that I would have to continue if I was to succeed in helping these monkeys and other animals in similar situations. 99** [4]

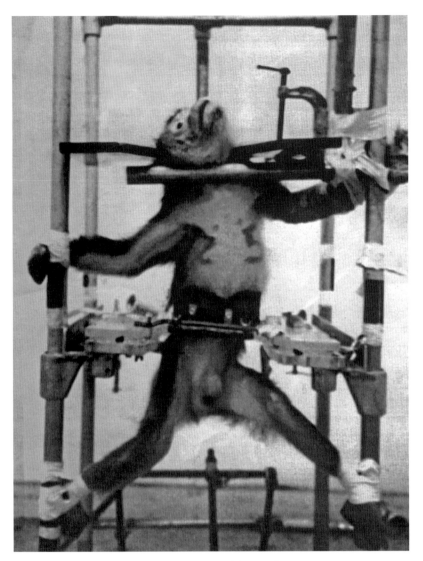

The monkeys in the lab were subjected to horrible experiments and conditions.

The state of the monkeys themselves was just as horrifying. Most of them had one or more surgically disabled limbs. Pacheco observed dozens of open wounds, none of which had been properly treated. Bandages were either nonexistent or filthy. Pacheco also realized most of the monkeys were neurotic. Some were spinning in their cages, others were banging on the walls, and some were even chewing on their own limbs.

Overwhelmed by the monkeys' living conditions, Pacheco sneaked fruit into the lab to supplement their inadequate diet. He held their hands to provide them with some of the physical affection they craved. He even began feeling guilty when he left them at night. Yet despite the horrible conditions, Pacheco said nothing to Taub. He believed if he complained, Taub would fire him and his undercover mission would be ruined.

PRIMATES AND HUMANS

Throughout history, most humans have considered themselves superior to all other species. This thinking led and still leads some people to allow the use of animals in research, as the monkeys were used in Silver Spring. But others have challenged that belief for centuries, including Carl Linnaeus in the 1700s. Through his work classifying organisms, Linnaeus claimed humans are primates, as are apes and monkeys.

In the 1800s, Charles Darwin formulated the theory of evolution, stating humans share a common ancestor with primates. In the 1970s, scientists hypothesized the common ancestor lived 20 million years ago. But modern methods of DNA comparison now show the common ancestor lived less than 4 million years ago.[5] Science further indicates humans share more than 90 percent of their genetic code with other primates.[6]

Taub admired what he thought was Pacheco's dedication. He soon assigned him a lead research position despite Pacheco's lack of experience. As part of the new position, Pacheco was given a set of keys to the lab. With the access the keys provided, Pacheco began documenting the lab conditions at night. He took video and photographs. He wrote pages of notes. And he even brought in veterinarians and scientists after hours to support his case. These five individuals signed affidavits attesting to the awful conditions of the lab.

Finally in September 1981, Pacheco took his evidence to the Montgomery County, Maryland, police. On September 11, the police raided the lab, entering with force. They seized the 17 monkeys. Taub was charged with 17 counts of animal cruelty. It marked the first time in history a federally funded researcher was charged with animal cruelty. It was also the first time in history research animals were confiscated.

THE CASE RESULTS

Once the police department filed charges, the NIH suspended Taub's funding. They required him to justify his spending and present research results. In district court, Taub was found guilty of six counts of animal cruelty for failing to provide needed medical care for six monkeys.

However, of the original 17 counts of animal cruelty, Taub was cleared on 11 charges. The court said the small cages, unsanitary conditions, and emotional suffering were not sufficient evidence of cruelty. Taub appealed the verdict on the remaining six counts. The circuit court overturned each conviction. The court claimed it could not apply Maryland's animal cruelty statute to a research institution working under a US federal program such as the NIH.

The fate of the monkeys was also at stake. When the police raided the IBR labs in

ANIMAL WELFARE ACT

The Silver Spring monkeys case exposed more than just the inhumane treatment of 17 monkeys. It also exposed the severe limitations of the 1970 Animal Welfare Act (AWA). The act was intended to regulate the use of animals for experimentation, education, and research. But as the Silver Spring monkeys' conditions illustrated in 1981, the law was severely flawed.

The primary focus of the AWA was preserving humans' rights to use animals, rather than protecting the animals' rights or even their safety in many cases. To that end, the act did not apply to many species, including cold-blooded animals, rats, mice, and farm animals. Also, individual researchers were not required to be licensed. Nor were experiments regulated. The law only called for the researchers to use acceptable standards of animal care, treatment, and use. Finally, the USDA and state agencies were not committed to enforcing the act's anticruelty statutes. Thus, while the AWA was a small step toward animal welfare, the law did not afford animals legal rights.

September 1981, they placed the 17 monkeys in PETA's care. But a few days after Taub's arrest, Taub's attorney prepared a motion for the return of the monkeys, which were Taub's property. The monkeys were returned to IBR. Within days, one monkey died in Taub's custody. After that, the judge ordered the monkeys to be placed at the NIH primate quarantine center in Maryland.

In the ensuing years, PETA waged war with the NIH, trying to secure the release of the monkeys. PETA even offered to place the monkeys in a sanctuary at PETA's expense. The NIH turned down the offer. Ultimately, the courts ruled PETA could not sue on behalf of the monkeys. In the end, five of the 17 monkeys were placed at the San Diego Zoo. The rest either died, were subjected to further experimentation, or were euthanized.

LASTING IMPACT

Even though the convictions were overturned, the case was still a small victory for animal rights. It was the first time police had cooperated with an animal rights organization and presented evidence at a trial. It was the first-ever conviction of a researcher on charges of animal cruelty. It sent a message that the scientific community and large institutions were not beyond scrutiny.

The case also thrust the animal rights movement into public view. Prior to the Silver Spring monkeys case, the public was largely unaware of what happened in research facilities. But after the case broke and throughout the years of legal battles, media coverage made the Silver Spring monkeys famous. PETA and other organizations used the campaign to show the public abuse was occurring in many research facilities. They also used it to rally public support for protests and marches. Likewise, members of Congress were called to action. Some politicians became involved in the custody battle over the monkeys after the police raid. Others joined forces to sponsor future legislation regarding animal welfare.

Finally, the Silver Spring monkeys case empowered PETA and the animal rights movement. Activists learned an in-depth investigation of a specific organization, precise goals, and

MAIL TO THE WHITE HOUSE

In the 1980s, concerned citizens flooded the White House with letters about the Silver Spring monkeys case. The case created the third-largest volume of mail to the White House that decade. Even in 1990, First Lady Barbara Bush received more than 43,000 letters about the monkeys.[7] The letters requested her assistance in freeing the monkeys still involved in a custody battle years after their 1981 seizure from the lab. The letters showed how the Silver Spring case—and the growing animal rights movement—had captured the public's attention. The letters also showed that many people inside as well as outside the movement were demanding change for animals.

relentless determination brought results. The case inspired animal rights activists to take legal action on behalf of animals. It set an early precedent as the animal rights movement would grow in the decades to come. ●

Alex Pacheco, seen here in 2011, inspired »
animal rights activists with his dedication to
the Silver Spring undercover investigation.

CHAPTER 2

ROOTS OF THE MOVEMENT

Throughout history, humans have had a relationship with animals. But within that relationship is a myriad of attitudes about animals. For centuries, philosophers and religious thinkers have argued many sides of the debate.

Some philosophers believed humans were unequivocally superior to animals. Thus, they felt animals' thoughts and feelings did not deserve consideration.

« **The animal welfare movement began in an effort to provide more humane care for workhorses hauling wagons and loads.**

Similarly, others subscribed to the conclusions of René Descartes, a French philosopher in the 1600s. He proposed animals were unfeeling creatures, or automatons. In contrast, many others felt animals were sentient, or capable of feeling pleasure and pain. They felt animals deserved compassion, respect, and moral rights.

In another philosophy, utilitarians advocated the use of animals, so long as the animals were cared for and their pain and distress were minimized. This approach is often referred to as animal welfare. Discussions about animal welfare entered public discourse in the late 1700s. Soon after, concerned animal advocates began to take decisive action to make animals' conditions more humane.

BEGINNINGS IN GREAT BRITAIN

One of the most famous quotes in the history of the animal welfare movement was from English philosopher Jeremy Bentham. He published *An Introduction to the Principles of Morals and Legislation* in 1789. He wrote, "The question is not, Can they reason? nor, Can they talk? but, Can they suffer?"[1] He was one of the first people in Western history to suggest animals may one day be granted legal rights because they are sentient beings. However, being a utilitarian, Bentham also defended

ELLA WHEELER WILCOX

Bentham is often credited with being the first to address the issue of animal suffering. As the humanitarian effort grew, more writers used their skills to bring attention to animal issues. One such writer and animal advocate was Ella Wheeler Wilcox. Knowing animals were unable to speak against the cruelty they endured, Wilcox created a voice for them in the early 1900s. Her poem "The Voice of the Voiceless" reads, "I am the voice of the voiceless; / Through me the dumb shall speak; / Till the deaf world's ear be made to hear / The cry of the wordless weak."[2] More than a century later, these lines are still quoted as the foundation for the mission to help animals.

the use of animals for food, so long as they did not suffer.

Many years after Bentham published *An Introduction to the Principles of Morals and Legislation*, Richard Martin came to the defense of animals. Martin, a member of the House of Commons in Great Britain, introduced into Parliament what is known as Martin's Act. The act was passed in 1822. It sought to prevent the cruel treatment of large domestic animals, which includes horses, cows, mules, oxen, steers, sheep, and more. The law also outlined the punishment for people caught beating or mistreating such animals. It was the first national animal protection law in Great Britain. In an effort to enforce the act, Martin proposed in 1824

A member of the **RSPCA** inspects a workhorse in 1880.

the formation of what is now known as the Royal Society for the Prevention of Cruelty to Animals (RSPCA).

IN THE UNITED STATES

People began taking action toward animal welfare in the United States after the American Civil War (1861–1865).

EARLY ANIMAL PROTECTION GROUPS

While the RSPCA in Great Britain generally gets credit for being the first animal protection organization, it has a predecessor. On October 25, 1809, the Liverpool Society for Preventing Wanton Cruelty to Brute Animals was established. The society angered haulers and carters, many of whom overworked and did not take care of their animals. The haulers thought the society might make them stop using the animals completely, leaving the haulers without a way to make a living. As a result, members of the society were forced to meet in secret for their own protection. Today the society is known as the RSPCA Liverpool Branch.

Wealthy former diplomat Henry Bergh was increasingly disturbed by how work animals were treated on the streets of New York City. After observing Britain's RSPCA, Bergh sought to create a similar organization in the United States. He wrote the "Declaration of the Rights of Animals." He appealed to many of New York's most prominent citizens to sign the declaration. With the support of many New Yorkers, Bergh formed the American Society for the Prevention of Cruelty to Animals (ASPCA) on April 10, 1866. After the ASPCA formed, similar organizations sprang up across the country. It marked the beginning of an organized animal welfare movement in the United States.

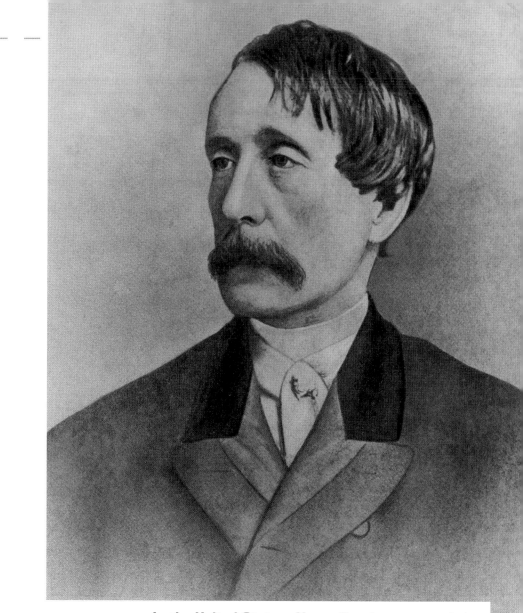

In the United States, Henry Bergh was one of the leading voices in the animal welfare movement.

Similar to Bergh, wealthy citizen Caroline Earle White witnessed the abuse of work animals on the streets. When she was a child in Philadelphia, these beatings so upset her she avoided certain streets altogether. As an adult, White cofounded the Pennsylvania Society for the Prevention of Cruelty to Animals (PSPCA). Because of male-dominated norms of the time, White was unable to hold an official position in the PSPCA, even though she cofounded it. Undeterred, she founded a women's branch of the organization. For similar reasons, several other women's groups formed across the country as well. In 1869, White's women's group created a refuge for lost and stray dogs in Philadelphia. It became the United States' first animal shelter and a model for urban animal control.

Bergh and White led the first US campaigns for animal welfare, fighting against the abuse of workhorses. Prior to automobiles, large animals such as horses were the engines of mass transit and

BLACK BEAUTY

As individuals strove to improve public awareness about animal abuse, Anna Sewell wrote the timeless classic *Black Beauty*. The story, told from the perspective of an abused horse, was originally published in 1890. It contrasted shameful human behavior with the dignity of a horse that could reason, reflect, grieve, and celebrate. The American Humane Education Society distributed more than 2 million free copies.[3] They hoped *Black Beauty* would do for animal welfare what the antislavery novel *Uncle Tom's Cabin* did for the abolition movement. It never reached the antislavery book's status. However, the book is still popular today.

transport. Yet many horses were overworked, abused, and underfed. Horse carcasses were common sights on city streets. In response, ASPCA water trucks patrolled New York streets, filling up fountains and delivering buckets of water to horses. The ASPCA also hosed down horses on hot days and created the first horse ambulance. Bergh himself was known for stopping drivers who whipped their horses. He caused many traffic jams as he stopped overloaded carts and unhitched weakened horses. He was even known to make citizen's arrests of those violating anticruelty statutes. Likewise in Philadelphia, White called for women to make citizen's arrests of abusers and to boycott companies that mistreated their

EDUCATION CAMPAIGNS

Early animal welfare activists recognized the need to raise public awareness about the abuses animals endured. As one way to do this, they launched education campaigns. The ASPCA introduced one of the first formal education programs in 1916. It was aimed at children, with the goal that they would grow up being kind to animals. By 1924, 23 states had implemented humane education in schools. Children were encouraged to begin their own clubs as well and to make a difference in the fight for animals.

Another education campaign is the American Humane Association's Be Kind to Animals Week. It first began in 1915 and grew considerably through 1945. It is still celebrated today. Over the years, supporters have celebrated the week by distributing literature, fundraising, holding special ceremonies, and more.

animals. While their work helped many horses, it was not appreciated by everyone. Often, Bergh and ASPCA agents were met with verbal abuse, threats, and even beatings.

LIVESTOCK CONCERNS

Bolstered by Bergh's and others' successes, animal activists sought to improve the treatment of livestock in the late 1800s. On a long trip to a slaughterhouse, animals such as cattle were crammed into railcars without the ability to lie down. They were denied both food and water. Once they reached the slaughterhouse, conditions worsened. Killing methods were imprecise, excruciating, and prolonged.

To begin their campaign, activist groups exposed the shocking details of how the emerging industry of agribusiness treated livestock. These farms were much different than the small family farms people typically envisioned. At a time when the public feared diseases, activists described the tuberculosis, cholera, infected wounds, and decomposing carcasses in the slaughterhouses. Exposing the cruelty and health risks earned activists public support to push for legislation regulating livestock transport. This resulted in the first federal anticruelty statute in the United States. The Twenty-Eight Hour Law of 1873 required that animals be

« **Activists raised awareness about the inhumane treatment of livestock, including crude killing methods.**

fed, watered, and rested every 28 hours. Enforcing the law was difficult, but it nonetheless set a precedent for animal welfare legislation.

Over the years, the animal welfare movement continued to thrive. But not everyone was satisfied with incremental steps merely to improve conditions for animals. They wanted more. Thus began the discussion of, and action toward, the abolition of the use of animals by humans. ●

**The Twenty-Eight Hour Law sought to improve conditions »
for livestock traveling on trains to slaughterhouses.**

CHAPTER 3

NEW VISIONS

By the late 1800s, animal welfare was a conversation topic in many middle- and upper-class circles. More and more people were taking public action on behalf of animals. The great majority of these efforts focused on the prevention of cruelty to animals. Many laws were enacted to this end. Yet the laws and accomplishments fell far short of ending animal suffering. As a result, the discussion about the treatment of animals evolved from one about animal welfare to one about abolishing the use of animals altogether.

VIVISECTION AND MEDICAL ADVANCEMENTS

In the late 1800s, vivisection, or the cutting into a live animal for the purpose of gaining scientific knowledge, was on the rise. As a result, doctors and scientists were gaining respect as their research yielded medical advances. Diphtheria mortality rates, for example, were considerably reduced as a result of the development of an antitoxin in 1894. Other advances made possible through vivisection included treatment for syphilis, smallpox, malaria, and other life-threatening

THE HISTORY OF VIVISECTION

The practice of using animals for experimentation dates back to ancient times. Galen, a Roman physician in the 100s CE, is the so-called father of vivisection. At the time, his work led to a greater understanding of health and disease. Even before that, in the 300s BCE, Greek philosopher Aristotle performed experiments on live animals. In the 1500s, Italian physicians expanded on Galen's findings. Then in the 1600s, an English physician used live animals to discover blood circulation throughout the body.

At the time, there was no anesthesia. Some physicians began to speak against vivisection because of the undue pain and suffering it caused. In response, in the 1600s, Descartes argued animals were unthinking and unfeeling. Not until Darwin published his research in the mid-1800s were Descartes's ideas scientifically challenged, which helped the antivivisection movement.

illnesses. Doctors were also able to improve surgical techniques. They likewise studied and learned more about tumors, abscesses, and brain disorders. Not all vivisection experiments led to such advancements, though. Many experiments were performed on animals entirely out of a curiosity about how living organisms worked. Others were performed without any medical foundation whatsoever. Nearly all were performed without anesthesia.

Regardless of the validity of the experiments or the advancements made, some people objected to using animals for such a purpose. Thus, the antivivisection

ABOLITIONIST PARALLELS

The antivivisection activists sought complete abolition of vivisection on animals. It was perhaps the first abolitionist campaign for animals. After the American Civil War, some animal activists drew parallels between the treatment of animals and the oppression of African-American slaves. Antislavery abolitionists challenged the belief that slaves were merely property to be bought, sold, and used. They also challenged the belief that slaves were not sentient beings, as some proslavery supporters believed.

Animal rights proponents used the lessons of the antislavery movement to challenge the institutional oppression of animals. First, they exposed the reality of animal abuse to the public through education, lectures, and pamphlets. Next, animal advocates took their cause into the political arena. And the ultimate goal of animal rights activists was, and still is, the emancipation of all animals, just as all slaves had been set free.

movement took root. These activists were among the first to argue for the abolition of the use of animals for human purposes.

ANTIVIVISECTION MOVEMENT

In 1883, White founded the American Anti-Vivisection Society (AAVS). The group worked to raise public awareness. They wanted people to consider the immorality of using animals for experiments. They wanted the public to understand the pain these animals suffered. Antivivisectionists cited example after example of subjects howling in pain. They used images depicting mutilated animals in dark cages. And they worked toward legislation to end vivisection. White asserted that using animal subjects for tests relating to human biology was unreliable. Similarly, others argued vivisection did little to contribute to medical knowledge.

However, the medical establishment undermined these arguments. Prominent doctors and scientists gave persuasive testimony about the benefits of vivisection. In an era plagued by disease, researchers had powerful arguments to continue using animals in laboratories. They argued antivivisectionists were against science as well as ignorant of it. Furthermore, doctors and scientists were nearly all men, while most antivivisectionists were women.

WOMEN IN THE ANTIVIVISECTION MOVEMENT

Many activists in the antivivisection movement were women, while scientists and doctors were almost entirely men. In the early 1900s, tension between the scientific community and antivivisectionists was growing. A respected neurologist labeled female antivivisectionists as victims of a disorder called "zoophil-psychosis." The diagnosis sought to explain what some felt was radical behavior from these female activists. The neurologist claimed women were weak by nature, which made them susceptible to a "psychotic love of animals."[1] According to the neurologist, men who fell victim to this psychosis could easily be treated with therapy, but women were nearly impossible to cure.

Traditional gender roles of the time gave more authority to men.

Nonetheless, antivivisectionists showed they were not afraid to challenge cultural norms and large institutions. Antivivisectionists exposed what they considered the immorality of animal experimentation. In doing so, they also called into question the integrity of doctors and scientists who were traditionally highly regarded in society. So while the antivivisection movement itself did not make significant advances until after World War II (1939–1945), it laid visionary groundwork for an animal rights movement in the United States.

Slowly but surely, the antivivisection movement spread across the globe.

A REVOLUTIONARY DIET

During the 1800s, animal welfare activists did not suggest people should stop eating meat entirely as a means to end slaughterhouse abuses. They merely worked for improved conditions for livestock. In contrast to this approach, other individuals committed to a life of vegetarianism, or a meatless diet.

Vegetarianism was not a new concept even in the 1800s. Greek philosopher Plutarch (46–120 CE) did not eat meat. He did so to show kindness to both humans and nonhumans. *Vegetarian* officially became an English word in 1842. The first known vegetarian society was formed in Great Britain in 1847. The ideology gained favor throughout that century. Well-known figures such as American writer Henry David Thoreau, Irish playwright George Bernard Shaw, and English author Henry Salt were vegetarians. Salt wrote *A Plea for Vegetarianism* in 1886. Many of these first vegetarians eliminated meat from their diets as a form of boycott. Their hope was that fewer animals would be raised for consumption. More important, these early vegetarians sought to put an end to the suffering of animals raised and slaughtered for food.

In the early 1900s, some people within the vegetarian movement began questioning the ethics of consuming dairy products as well as meat. They questioned whether using a cow for its milk was any

HENRY SALT

More and more in the 1800s, animal advocacy became a topic of public discourse. Most conversations focused on animal welfare, with the notion that animals should be treated "with care, kindness and compassion."[2] But in 1892, Englishman Henry Salt published *Animals' Rights Considered in Relation to Social Progress*, sparking a debate over animal rights. Salt contended that rights are not a privilege reserved only for human beings. He predicted the future would bring more protections to more animals. He also claimed that one day, society would see similarities in the false reasons to justify slavery and the reasons used to deny animals rights. In addition, Salt wrote *A Plea for Vegetarianism* in 1886. Indian independence leader Mohandas Gandhi credited his commitment to vegetarianism to Salt's work.

In the 1800s, several famous figures became vegetarians, including American author Henry David Thoreau.

less exploitive than using it for its meat. They called themselves "non-dairy vegetarians."[3] In November 1944, the Vegan Society was founded to end the exploitation of animals and take the ideology even further. Their mission is "Promoting ways of living free from animal products for the benefit of people, animals and the environment."[4] The society promoted veganism, which is a diet without the consumption of any animal products, including milk, eggs, or honey. In the 1970s, when the modern animal rights movement fully emerged, both vegetarianism and veganism would become more mainstream practices. ●

**As more people enjoyed meatless diets, »
a vegetarian restaurant attracted many
patrons in Paris in the early 1900s.**

CHAPTER 4

IDEOLOGY INTO ACTION

T he antivivisection movement in the late 1800s and early 1900s pioneered the concept of completely abolishing humans' exploitation of animals. Vegetarians and vegans began to show others how to personally stop using animals for food. For decades, these and other ideologies grew and spread. Then in the 1970s, philosophers took significant steps to define the idea of animal rights. New, stronger viewpoints sparked new, stronger action.

ANIMAL LIBERATION

The idea of animal rights significantly evolved following the 1975 publication of *Animal Liberation* by Australian philosopher Peter Singer. It is heralded as one of the most influential books in the animal rights movement. Singer asserts that, from an ethical standpoint, animals should be considered equal to humans. He holds that just as race and sex are not justifications for different treatment, neither is species. Therefore, the way most humans treat animals "is not justified simply because we are one species and they are another."[1] Singer explains how ethics shaped his arguments:

> *The premise of* Animal Liberation *is simply that the way in which we separate humans from animals, ethically speaking, that is put them in a different ethical sphere, is not really justified just by the fact that we're one species and they're another.*[2]

He concludes, then, that nothing justifies the idea that animals are simply objects available for human use. Singer's book also exposes the inhumane treatment of animals used for food and research. Further, he maintains that the choices most people made in everyday life support

SPECIESISM

In 1970, Richard Ryder, an animal rights activist, wrote "Speciesism," an essay leaflet. Ryder coined the term *speciesism*, which parallels such words as *racism* and *sexism*. In 1975, Singer popularized the term in *Animal Liberation*. He further defined *speciesism* as "a prejudice or attitude of bias in favor of the interests of members of one's own species and against those of members of other species."[4] The term was added to the *Oxford English Dictionary* in 1985.

"shocking forms of cruelty."[3]

Animal Liberation forced many people to take a closer look at their personal habits and cultural norms based on the idea of human superiority. It called into question everything people considered about animals. And it brought the ideas of moral rights and the liberation of animals into the public arena. This ideology propelled many to a new level of activism in the name of animal rights.

SPIRA TAKES ACTION

As animal rights moved into the public spotlight in the mid-1970s, more and more people took action. One such person was Henry Spira, a New York high school English teacher. He read *Animal Liberation* and attended one of Singer's classes at New York University. Spira said, "Singer made an enormous impression on me because his concern for other animals was rational and defensible in public debate. It did not depend on sentimentality."[5] Spira was inspired. He is one of the activists credited with helping mobilize the modern animal rights movement from philosophy to action.

Spira focused his efforts on ending animal experimentation and raising public awareness about the issue. He specifically targeted experiments the average person would deem appalling, especially those involving beloved animals such as cats and dogs. In 1975, he discovered an experiment researchers were conducting in

PHILOSOPHICAL DIFFERENCES

As the animal rights movement emerged in the 1970s, it did so separately from the established animal welfare movement. There are many differences in their ideologies and strategies. The welfare movement works for the humane treatment of animals. As utilitarians, welfarists accept human use of animals as long as animals are safeguarded against unnecessary pain and suffering. Welfarists promote compassion for animals and work for reform in existing systems as a means to protect animals. A notable welfare group is the Humane Society of the United States.

In contrast, the animal rights movement "demands justice, equality, fairness and rights."[6] Rightists also argue animals are sentient beings, deserving of ethical consideration and freedom from human exploitation. To achieve this goal, they seek fundamental changes in attitude and action at both the individual and societal levels. Rightists denounce the use of animals for food, sport, clothing, research, entertainment, and any other human use.

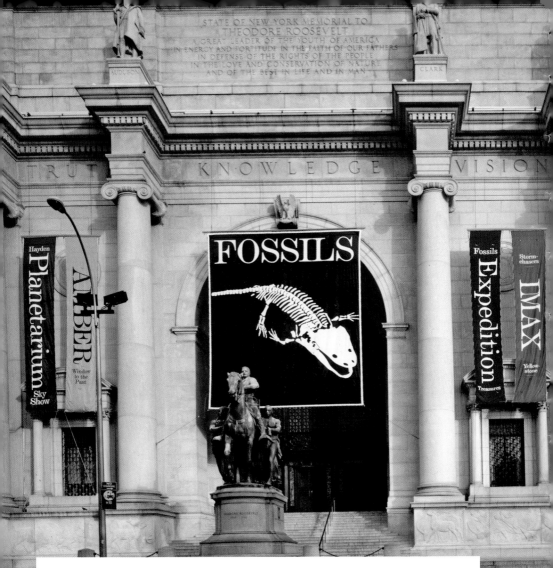

Henry Spira's first campaign targeted the American Museum of Natural History in New York City.

laboratories at New York's American Museum of Natural History. The experiment involved the deliberate, painful maiming of cats in order to study the effects on the cats' sexual behavior. While the researchers felt it was a valid study, Spira argued it did nothing to serve the greater good.

Working with other animal activists, Spira began a phone and letter campaign to museum officials. When his calls and letters went unanswered, Spira went to the media. He gave a detailed account of the experiments and how the museum had failed to respond to the concerns. Spira hoped the museum's experiments would strike an emotional chord with the general public—especially with millions of cat owners.

As he had expected, the public joined the cause. The museum and the NIH (which funded the experiments, as it had in the Silver Spring monkeys case) were overwhelmed with protest letters. Nonetheless, the lab stayed in operation. Spira and others from animal protection organizations then staged demonstrations on the steps of the museum every Saturday for a year and a half.

At one point, Congressman Ed Koch took interest in the campaign. He toured the laboratory and personally questioned researchers about the validity and necessity of the test. He received no answer. In addition, because the NIH was a federal agency, Koch was concerned about the test's purpose because US taxpayers were paying for it. Koch took his concerns back to Congress, and 120 members joined him in questioning spending money

Spira's protest against the museum attracted public attention because many people consider cats beloved pets.

on such experiments. Finally, the NIH withdrew funding. At the end of 1977, the museum ceased the experiments.

This was not simply a victory for the museum cats. It was a win for the animal rights movement as a whole.

Spira had successfully targeted a high-profile laboratory, created a coalition of activists, and garnered support from public figures. As Singer explained,

> *It was the first time that a campaign against experiments on animals actually succeeded in stopping a series of experiments, and it showed that it was possible to make progress, as long as the campaign was based on good evidence and aimed at a vulnerable target.*[7]

CATS

One of the reasons Henry Spira targeted the American Museum of Natural History in New York was because it used cats in its research labs, and he recognized that would strike an emotional chord with millions of cat owners.

Human adoration of cats dates back to ancient Egypt, where archaeologists unearthed a cat cemetery of more than 300,000 cat mummies. In addition, killing a cat in Egypt was often penalized by death. Ancient Romans held a comparable admiration for cats, as they were considered a symbol of liberty. And in the Far East, people valued cats because they protected documents from unscrupulous rodents.

In the modern United States, cats are claimed to be the favorite pet, and in 2007, more than 90 million cats ruled the roost in approximately 34 percent of American homes.[8]

RABBITS AT REVLON

Following the success of the museum campaign, Spira turned his attention to a situation involving a greater number of animals. In 1979, he targeted the Draize test. In this procedure, researchers tested cosmetics and other products on rabbits to determine the products' irritancy to eyes and skin. The widely used test blinded and killed millions of rabbits. Once again, Spira researched the issue before taking action. He concluded the tests were unnecessary and subjective, and they needlessly inflicted suffering on the animals. Spira was not the only one opposed to the test. Even some animal researchers were critical of it.

Spira chose a highly visible target: Revlon, a large, well-known cosmetics company that used the Draize test. He began by writing letters requesting a meeting. Spira wanted to start a dialogue to persuade Revlon to put a percentage of their earnings into research for nonanimal alternatives to the Draize test. For more than a year, Revlon refused to talk to Spira.

Next, Spira built a coalition of more than 400 organizations.[9] It was unlike any other coalition previously seen in the animal rights movement. The coalition placed graphic ads in newspapers to show the public what Revlon did behind closed doors. "We could juxtapose the dream of beauty that they were fashioning, with the reality nightmare of the rabbits," said Spira.[10]

Within months, Revlon agreed to donate $75,000 to Rockefeller University researchers developing nonanimal

VOICES
OF THE
MOVEMENT

Henry Spira was one of the first to show how to turn philosophy into action in order to create change on behalf of animals:

"Basically, the strategy for all freedom fights or struggles against injustice is similar. The other side has the power, but we have justice on our side, and justice can mobilize people. We need to draw on all available energy and expertise. We need to work out our short-term goals so that we can reach people and eventually bring about fundamental change.

The victories we have achieved show that citizen activism can succeed even against prestigious scientific institutions, multi-national corporations and inert bureaucracies." [11]

Spira's activism reduced the number of rabbits being used in cosmetic product testing.

testing alternatives. Within a few years, Revlon had also reduced the number of animals it used in testing by 50 percent.[12] Building on the momentum, Spira then approached other large cosmetics companies, including Avon. In order to avoid the public relations nightmare Revlon experienced, each company quickly contributed funds to explore alternatives to animal experimentation.

Some activists criticized Spira, however, for not fighting each corporation until it abolished animal experimentation altogether. Spira believed, though, that in order to achieve change he had to establish common goals with the opposition. He later turned his attention to animals raised for food. Spira campaigned against the USDA, McDonald's, poultry processing company Perdue, and Kentucky Fried Chicken until his death in 1998. He was credited with accomplishing "more for animals than any organization or person had in the past century."[13] His tactics and successes provided valuable lessons for the expanding animal rights movement. ●

THE GROWTH OF VEGETARIANISM

As thinkers and activists better defined the animal rights philosophy, the number of vegetarians increased in the 1970s. Similar to their Vegan Society counterparts formed in 1944, the North American Vegetarian Society (NAVS) advocates "healthy, compassionate and ecological living."[14] Founded in 1974, the group believes a vegetarian diet is not only healthier for humans but it also promotes more humane treatment of animals. In 1976, the NAVS organized their first Vegetarian Summerfest, a conference that educates attendees about vegetarian lifestyles. It is one of the largest gatherings of both vegetarians and vegans in the United States.

CHAPTER 5

THE MOVEMENT TAKES OFF

Building on the ideology and progress of the 1970s, the 1980s saw dramatic growth in the animal rights movement. Countless animal rights organizations were born. By the end of the decade, several national and international groups had emerged. In addition, hundreds of smaller, local organizations formed across the United States.

« As hundreds of animal rights groups formed in the 1980s, activism increased and drew public attention.

The groups represented a myriad of issues, from animal experimentation to killing animals for fur. Some focused on a single form of animal exploitation, such as vivisection or factory farms. Still other groups formed to end hunting. Groups of professionals, including veterinarians, physicians, and even actors, also organized.

The groups differed in tactics as well as focus. Some organizations fought for animals in court, while others worked to raise awareness of animal issues. Sanctuaries were also created to provide a safe environment for

ANTIFuR CAMPAIGN

Perhaps one of the most notable campaigns in the 1980s was against Canadian seal hunting. Each year, hundreds of thousands of seal pups were clubbed to death for their pure-white fur. Several groups, including the Fund for Animals and environmental group Greenpeace, created an international coalition against the hunt. These groups shuttled reporters and photographers to remote locations to document the slaughter. Activists were often arrested, fined, and jailed. Some even faced attacks from hunters.

Despite a public outrage, the Canadian hunt continued due to a demand for fur. Outside Canada, however, the European Commission banned the import of seal fur in 1983. In 2009, the European Union voted to ban trade of products from commercial seal hunts. Also in 2009, US Senate Resolution 84 called for an immediate end to the hunt. Yet despite international opposition, the hunt continues. Today, millions participate in Fur-Free Friday in an effort to call attention to the ongoing slaughter of seals.

abused, rescued animals. A few groups even turned to more aggressive tactics, including vandalizing laboratories, abducting lab animals, setting birds free, harassing hunters in the woods, and more. And while all these groups remained mostly disconnected from one another, they worked toward the same overarching goal of animal rights.

PETA

Formed in 1980, PETA is one of the best-known animal rights groups. After firsthand exposure to animal suffering, Newkirk and Pacheco formed PETA as a grassroots organization. While it wanted to end the suffering of all animals at the hands of humans, PETA focused on animals used for research, food, entertainment, and fur. PETA's membership began at less than 20 members in 1980.[1] Membership grew to more than 300,000 in less than a decade.[2] In 2013, it had more than 3 million members.[3] PETA's focus is on areas in which the greatest "numbers of animals suffer the most intensely for the longest periods of time: on factory farms, in the clothing trade, in laboratories, and in the entertainment industry."[4] They do so through education, undercover work, public demonstrations, legislation, and more.

In 1981, PETA members were energized by their success in the Silver Spring monkeys case. In another campaign, PETA took on the University of Pennsylvania

Head Injury Lab. The lab, headed by Thomas Gennarelli, received approximately $1 million per year to study head injuries. The study's test subjects were baboons, and the methods were quite controversial. In May 1984, PETA received videotapes the Animal Liberation Front (ALF) had stolen. The ALF also damaged Gennarelli's lab during the break-in. The video had been recorded by researchers in the lab and was never intended to be released to the public. The tapes revealed baboons receiving numerous powerful blows to the head, operations without anesthesia in unsterile conditions, and a callous research team.

DUMP GILLETTE

After the Silver Spring monkeys case, PETA launched another undercover investigation. In 1986, group members released videotape of the Gillette Company cosmetics testing lab, where animals were used. Gillette indeed shut down that lab. But they then set up testing at an independent lab, making surveillance difficult.

Relentless, PETA launched the Dump Gillette campaign. They urged consumers to send products back to the company for a refund. Even singer Paul McCartney, formerly of the music group the Beatles, boycotted Gillette. Working with his wife, Linda, McCartney was an outspoken vegetarian and animal activist. His celebrity sparked a great deal of media attention for the campaign. He reportedly returned his razor, shaving cream, and other Gillette products. He demanded a refund, which he then donated to PETA.

Gennarelli surveys the damage to his research lab after the ALF break-in.

PETA contacted the Pennsylvania Department of Health and Human Services, which oversaw the lab. They offered the department an opportunity to see the tapes and address the issue without public involvement. When the department declined the offer, PETA used the tapes to create *Unnecessary Fuss*, a 30-minute documentary. The title was based on Gennarelli's statement that PETA's campaign was just "unnecessary fuss" from overly sensitive activists.[5] The documentary spared nothing and horrified viewers into action.

Despite the public outcry, PETA was unable to stop the experiments with the documentary alone. The group took the case to Congress. As with the Silver Spring monkeys case, congressional members were moved to act on behalf of the animals, yet no results were achieved. PETA, still not willing to back down, staged a sit-in at the lab. After four days, the Pennsylvania Department of Health and Human Services finally suspended funds to Gennarelli's lab. Eventually, the lab closed. Once again, a PETA campaign had made the public aware of what happened inside laboratories that used animals for research.

FARM

While PETA challenged abuses against animals in research labs, other organizations in the 1980s fought abuses against animals raised for food.

THE OPPOSITION

Any movement that challenges the status quo faces opposition. In the animal rights movement, much of the opposition comes from groups that profit from the use of animals. With money, education, and lobbying, anti–animal rights efforts seek to portray the animal rights movement as a threat to cultural norms. Biomedical industries began their opposition to animal rights during the antivivisection movement. Their efforts continue on many fronts.

The beef, egg, and dairy industries are among the strongest anti–animal rights groups. The American Farm Bureau Federation, for example, developed a committee in 1982 specifically to deal with criticism from animal rights groups. They also actively lobby against legislation that they feel threatens their business.

The prohunting lobby, which includes the National Rifle Association, also presents a significant obstacle for animal rights organizations. It is one of the wealthiest lobbying organizations in the nation and continues challenging animal rights groups' antihunting campaigns.

Factory farming increased as demand for meat and eggs increased in US postwar society. Factory farming is an agribusiness, and the animals raised for food are often subjected to inhumane treatment.

Farm Animal Reform Movement (FARM), now called Farm Animal Rights Movement, was founded in July 1981. The group's goal was to stop the raising and killing of animals for food. Founder Alex Hershaft realized, though, the need to take small, incremental steps toward that long-term goal. As the FARM Web site states, "This is FARM's 'pragmatic abolitionist' approach."[6] The smaller goals focused on increasingly improving conditions for farm animals. Hershaft identified the four phases of a successful campaign: a public alert about the

GREAT AMERICAN MEATOUT

On March 20, 1985, FARM organized the first Great American Meatout. It was modeled on the Great American Smokeout, an American Cancer Society campaign encouraging smokers to quit for at least one day. FARM encouraged meat eaters to forgo meat and animal products for one day—and then ideally for a lifetime. FARM's goal was to show people a meat-free diet is not only satisfying but it promotes personal health, protects the environment, and does not harm animals.

Since 1985, the Great American Meatout has become the world's largest "diet education campaign."[7] Every year on March 20, Meatout events around the world include information, cooking demonstrations, festivals, and more.

In the early 1980s, FARM led a campaign to ban veal crates, which severely restrict calves' movement.

problem, discussion, public acceptance of the problem, and legislative reform.

FARM's first effort was the veal ban campaign in 1981. Veal is meat from young calves. In order to produce the lean veal desired by consumers, factory farms use "veal crates" to restrict the young calves' movement. Farmers remove calves from their mothers, sometimes at only one day old, and place them in crates not much larger than the calves themselves. The calves can only stand or lie down.

To stave off restlessness, the calves are frequently kept in the dark 22 hours a day.[8]

FARM created advertisements showing the extreme conditions for veal calves. They also picketed restaurants serving veal. The campaign had short- and long-term effects. Once the public saw the shocking ads, veal sales fell dramatically and never rebounded.

THE CASE FOR ANIMAL RIGHTS

As more animal rights organizations were taking action in the early 1980s, the movement also saw a major development in ideology. Eight years after the publication of Singer's *Animal Liberation*, American philosopher Tom Regan published *The Case for Animal Rights* in 1983. Similar to Singer, Regan discusses justice and morality toward animals. But Regan took greater steps to establish himself as a rights-based activist.

While studying the philosophies of Indian activist Mohandas Gandhi, Regan began questioning his choice to eat meat. He contemplated whether the fork at his dinner table was an instrument of violence: "I had been so encultured as to not even think there was a moral question about eating animals."[9] To that end, Regan argues any human use of animals that causes suffering is morally wrong and should be eliminated. He calls for the complete abolition of using animals in both science and agriculture

VOICES OF THE MOVEMENT

Philosopher Tom Regan discusses how culture shapes people to form limiting viewpoints about animals:

❝I think the vast majority of people who really do care about their companion animals and don't think about other animals . . . are products of their culture, of their time, and place and circumstances. Our culture imprints this on us. . . . It teaches us that there is this categorical difference between the animals we eat and the animals we play with, the animals we wear and the animals that we sleep with, the animals that are part of our family and the animals who are pieces of dead flesh in cellophane wrapping.❞[10]

and the elimination of hunting and trapping. His beliefs challenged animal rights activists to confront the existing social structures and major institutions that support the abuse of animals.

Led by an even stronger ideology, animal rights groups did not slow down as the 1980s came to an end. PETA, FARM, and other organizations would continue to grow in size and influence into the 1990s and beyond. ●

**Since the 1980s, PETA cofounder Ingrid »
Newkirk has led demonstrations to draw
media attention to animal rights causes.**

PETA

CHAPTER 6

GAINING MOMENTUM

The animal rights movement continued growing into the 1990s. Activists—and the public—could see more and more evidence of the movement's influence. There was a reduction of consumer demand for fur, a reduction of the number of animals cosmetic companies used for testing, and even an increase in the number of vegetarians in the United States. It signaled an awakening of public awareness and support for the animal rights movement.

MARCH FOR THE ANIMALS

The animal rights movement was growing not just in terms of influence and awareness. It was also growing in the sheer number of people joining the cause. This was never more apparent than on June 10, 1990, when an estimated 25,000 animal rights activists gathered in Washington, DC, for the March for the Animals.[1] The event brought together a myriad of animal rights supporters. Some wanted to end experimentation on animals. Others wanted to see changes on factory farms. Still others wanted protections for certain species.

The demonstration was the largest in the history of animal advocacy. They gathered at a park near the White House and marched three miles to the US Capitol to draw attention to the plight of animals. They wanted both the public and the federal government to take notice. As participants walked the streets of Washington, they chanted, "What do we want? Animal rights! When do we want it? Now!"[2] Many demonstrators also carried banners and posters with animal rights slogans: "Animals are not for wearing," "Animals Have Rights, Too," and "Fur is Dead."[3] The weekend also included information

ANIMAL CRASH TESTS

With the movement in full force in the early 1990s, PETA targeted automobile manufacturer General Motors (GM). GM still used live animals, such as pigs and baboons, for automobile crash tests. Nonanimal alternatives to crash testing were certainly available at the time. All other car companies used computer testing models and state-of-the-art crash dummies.

PETA claimed GM used more than 20,000 animals (mice, rats, pigs, and rabbits) in its labs and in crash tests, causing undue torment.[5] The group staged protests to embarrass the company. Outside the International Auto Show in 1992, three PETA members in costume (two rabbits and a mouse) smashed a GM vehicle to bits. In 1993, GM quit using live animals in crash tests.

booths, workshops, performances, and other activities. The speakers were some of the most influential leaders in the animal rights movement: Singer, Regan, Newkirk, Pacheco, Hershaft, and others.

The march was considered a success by the animal rights movement. Peter Linck, one of the rally's organizers, believed the march showed the world what the animal rights movement is truly about. "The animal rights movement has arrived, and we're not going away," Linck said.[4]

THE THREE *R*s

Long before the animal rights movement was in full swing in the 1990s, two British scientists, W. M. S. Russell and

Rex Burch, published *The Principles of Humane Experimental Technique* in 1959. In it, the scientists outlined alternatives to using animals for experimentation. They called their concept "the three Rs": replacement, reduction, and refinement.[6] Replacement urged fellow scientists to use nonsentient materials such as tissue or cells instead of animals in tests. Reduction encouraged them to use a minimal number of animals to obtain testing results. Finally, refinement challenged researchers to redesign experiments to minimize suffering and distress.

JENIFER GRAHAM AND FROG DISSECTION

Before the three *R*s made an impact in the scientific community, a single high school student was taking action on her own. In 1987, Jenifer Graham, a California high school student, refused to dissect a frog in biology class. While vivisection is performed on a still-living animal, dissection is performed on a preserved animal typically killed for the purpose. When Jenifer was threatened with a lower grade, she sued the school with her mother's support. In 1988, a district court judge ruled the school could still require her to participate in dissection, but only with a frog that had died of natural causes.

Jenifer's case empowered other students to take a stand against dissection. It also prompted further legal action giving students the right to refuse dissection on moral or religious grounds. That same year, California passed a law requiring schools to provide alternatives to dissection. Today, there are numerous options for students, including computer simulations, clay models, and much more.

In 1959, Russell and Burch's ideas were quickly dismissed by the scientific community. In the 1970s, antivivisectionists resurrected their ideas as alternatives to animal testing. And then in the 1990s, the timing was finally right for the concept to make a major impact. With joint efforts from animal advocacy groups, increased public awareness and media attention, and vast improvements in technology, the three *R*s entered the political arena. The NIH Revitalization Act of 1993 ordered the NIH to "develop, validate, and support tests that fulfill the three *R*s."[7]

As the scientific community began exploring the three *R*s, researchers realized nonanimal methods were usually less time consuming and less expensive than animal testing. Moreover, nonanimal testing often produced more accurate results. Today, nonanimal alternatives are increasingly accepted and explored by the scientific community. Rather than performing tests on living animals, many scientists perform tests in vitro. In vitro testing involves working with biological components outside of their environment, such as in a test tube. For example, human skin tissue created in vitro is used in burn research, cosmetic testing, and radiation exposure studies. In vitro procedures at the National Cancer Institute eliminate the use of approximately 6 million mice per year.[8]

Millions of mice are used every year in research labs, a number that can be reduced with the three *R*s.

Modern technology also serves as a replacement for animal experimentation. Now 95 percent of US medical schools use computer body simulators for training.[9] In some veterinary schools, plastic, soft-tissue organ models are used to teach beginning surgery. These models replace dogs that historically were used. Technology has also allowed scientists to study the human brain down to a single neuron through the use of brain imaging.

Finally, the environments in which laboratory animals are housed have been enriched in many facilities. Animals may now engage in more normal behavior, thus alleviating boredom and isolation. To reduce stress and suffering, many animals now receive pain-relieving medication.

The number of animals used for experimentation has been dramatically reduced due to public pressure as well as the acceptance by the scientific community that nonanimal alternatives are most often cheaper, faster, and more accurate. However, the use of animals as test subjects has not been completely eliminated. Animal rights activists are still working toward total abolition of the use of animals for research and science.

Into the new millennium, many activists in the growing movement stayed

IN VITRO MEAT

As the search for nonanimal alternatives in research gained acceptance, the question arose: are there alternatives to meat from living animals? Science shows that in vitro meat may, in fact, be a viable option. Scientists are working to create meat protein in labs. The in vitro meat can be grown controlling the amount of fat. Also, meat grown in laboratories would be produced in sterile conditions, free of the animal-borne diseases that sicken thousands yearly.

The animal rights movement ultimately promotes veganism to abolish the use of animals for food. Still, there is some interest in in vitro meat. In theory, it would eliminate the suffering of 47 billion animals raised and slaughtered annually for food. To encourage the idea, PETA offered a $1 million reward to the first scientist to develop in vitro meat.[10]

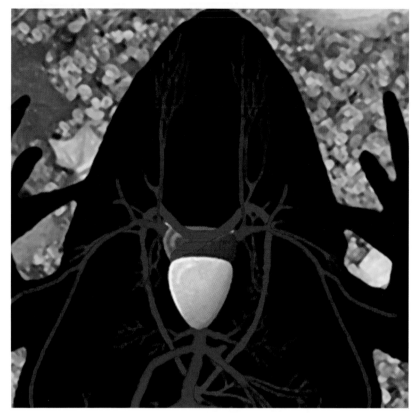

Dissection replacements such as digital diagrams bring activists closer to their goal of abolishing all animal experimentation.

focused on animals used for experimentation. Others turned the momentum to a new focus, where an even greater number of animals suffered. ●

CHAPTER 7

FOCUS ON FARMING

Without a doubt, the focus of the animal rights movement in the new millennium has been factory farming. Other campaigns still continue, but from the perspective of most advocates, the greatest amount of animal suffering is occurring on factory farms. It has become the major issue of public awareness campaigns and legislative attention.

Animal rights activists know most people have been brought up to believe farming is wholesome and humane. Most have pleasant images of family farms, with cows grazing on rolling green hills, chickens strutting about, and pigs rolling happily in the mud. Those farms are, for the most part, a thing of the past. Instead, most of today's farms are literally factories designed for mass production, and the product is animals for food. More than 19,000 animals are killed for food every minute in the United States.[1]

Not only are the numbers of animals raised and killed on factory farms each year staggering, but so is the treatment of the animals. What goes on inside windowless, remote sheds on industrial farms is kept far out of the reach of public consciousness. "People don't truly understand what is happening on these factory farms," says Gene Baur, president and cofounder of Farm Sanctuary, an organization that takes in thousands of abused farm animals.[2] One of the greatest obstacles is the enormous economic and political power of agribusiness in the United States.

Factory farming has proven to be a great challenge for the animal rights movement. The movement's first goal is to educate people about how those animals live and die. But the ultimate goal is to end factory farming and the

VOICES
OF THE
MOVEMENT

On December 5, 2012, Patricia Haddock, president of lobbyist group Delaware Votes For Animals, addressed the importance of factory farming as the key campaign of today's animal rights movement:

"The movement's emphasis today is on the farmed animals today . . . it is because of the sheer, staggering numbers. While we of course continue to advocate for companion animals [pets], laboratory animals, marine animals, wildlife, etc. it is the farmed animals who suffer some of the most intense suffering, and by far in the greatest numbers . . . by the billions. And while many people have yet to make the connection, these are animals that have the same feelings as our dogs and cats at home. Recent emerging science in the fields of animal sentience, intelligence, behavior, and animal emotions confirm this. Thus, the emphasis you will see in so many of the key leaders in the movement today on ending the cruelty to farmed animals."[3]

use of all animals being raised for food. It is an immense goal that cannot be achieved in one step. But animal rights groups are working toward it nonetheless.

FIRST LEGISLATION

Some animal rights activists have adopted a deliberately pragmatic approach to achieve steps such as legislation that improves conditions on farms. For example, one of the first campaigns against factory farming addressed the inhumane confinement of animals.

Factory farming began in the 1920s after the discovery of vitamins A and D. These vitamins were added to livestock feed. That meant animals no longer required exercise and sunlight for proper growth. Rather than keeping livestock in pastures, many farmers now kept them inside buildings. The discovery of antibiotics was also a factor that allowed the move to factory farms after World War II. Antibiotics prevented disease deaths in animals living tightly packed together. In addition, the development of assembly-line techniques for milking, egg collection, feeding, slaughter, and the like increased productivity. These methods also reduced operating costs for farmers.

One of the many abuses factory farm animals suffer is confinement inside these buildings. In the pork industry, for example, pregnant sows are often kept in

SANCTUARIES

When animals were rescued from abuse, such as from factory farms, activists needed somewhere to shelter them. In response to this need, some groups created sanctuaries for abused animals.

Farm Sanctuary was founded in 1986 in reaction to the growth of factory farming. Since then, the organization has provided homes for thousands of abused farm animals on its three different farms. It has grown to become "the largest and most effective farm animal rescue organization."[5] Other sanctuaries, such as the Black Beauty Ranch, take on a broader range of animals. Founded in 1979 by Cleveland Amory, the ranch provides safe homes for bison, cattle, horses, antelope, apes, camels, llamas, and more.

gestation crates, which are cages that are not even wide enough for them to turn around or lie down comfortably. Additionally, piglets are removed from their mothers shortly after birth, the sows are impregnated again, and the cycle continues. Farmers argue the crates reduce aggressive behavior and allow the sows to be fed according to individual needs.

In 2002, citizens in Florida introduced a ballot initiative to ban gestation crates. At the polls, 2.5 million voters voted in favor of the ban, effectively creating an amendment to their state constitution.[4] This was the first legislation in US history limiting the confinement of farm animals. By 2012, eight other states had followed Florida's lead

In landmark legislation, Florida was the first state to ban gestation crates that restricted sows.

and banned gestation crates. Fast-food chains Burger King and Wendy's pledged to purchase their pork only from suppliers that do not use gestation crates. Several of the nation's largest pork producers phased out the use of gestation crates due to such public and corporate pressure.

While the legislation was not a final goal by any means, it empowered animal rights activists to continue working in their efforts against factory farms.

McCRUELTY CAMPAIGN

In the late 1990s, PETA corresponded with the McDonald's company in an effort to get the company to demand changes at the factory farms and slaughterhouses that supplied the fast-food chain. Abuses and injuries of the chickens included bruises, broken bones, bleeding, and even painful methods of killing conscious birds. McDonald's ignored PETA's request. In 1999, PETA launched its McCruelty campaign. It included the slogan "I'm hating it" and a logo of Ronald McDonald wielding a knife.[6]

After more than 400 protests against McDonald's, the company agreed to make changes.[7] It marked the first time in the United States a meat seller agreed to make improvements on behalf of farm animals. After the initial improvements, PETA attempted to work with McDonald's to make further changes, but the fast-food chain refused. PETA relaunched the McCruelty campaign in February 2009. At the end of 2012, the campaign was ongoing.

PROPOSITION 2

In California, the largest animal agriculture state, animal rights groups worked to get a measure on the November 2008 ballot that would prohibit the severe confinement of all farm animals. The proposed law would require farmers to provide their animals with enough space to stand up, lie down, turn around, and stretch. The Prevention of Farm Animal Cruelty Act, known as Proposition 2, was officially added to the ballot with the help of 800,000 signatures, the majority collected by volunteers.[8]

In an effort to bring attention to Proposition 2, a broad coalition came together to support the measure. The coalition included animal rights and animal welfare groups, environmental organizations, veterinarian associations, and others. It was one of the largest coalitions ever formed in an anti–factory farming campaign.

Agribusiness, however, viewed the measure as one of the most threatening changes ever promoted by animal rights groups. Animal agriculture groups were so threatened by the measure that they believed they were in a fight to save their industry. Further, they felt if the proposition passed in California a domino effect would ensue, leading to similar regulations across the country.

UNDERCOVER INVESTIGATIONS

Prior to the November vote, Mercy for Animals (MFA), an organization focused on farm animal rights, went undercover from August to September at one of California's biggest factory egg farms. The goal was to "expose the routine abuse that takes place behind the closed doors of our nation's egg industry."[9] The undercover investigator was hired as a maintenance worker in the chicken barns. In addition to extreme confinement, the investigator witnessed sick birds left to die in piles, workers swinging birds around by the neck, open wounds on chickens that were never treated, hen corpses in cages together with live birds still laying eggs for human consumption, and more. Nathan Runkle, MFA founder and executive director, read reports and viewed video footage after this and other undercover investigations. He responded,

This is abuse that is so horrific, that if we kept dogs or cats in these conditions, it would be illegal. The very least that we can do in a civilized society is afford this basic protection to farm animals, as well.[10]

MERCY FOR ANIMALS

At age 11, Nathan Runkle came across literature on factory farming. The information led him to become a vegetarian, then later a vegan. At 13, Nathan attended the Animal Rights National Conference. He founded Mercy for Animals two years later, in 1999, at age 15. Since its inception, MFA has become one of the most effective groups at exposing animal cruelty. It also promotes veganism and educates the public about animal issues.

In addition to numerous well-known undercover investigations, Runkle and MFA work closely with a wide variety of groups and individuals for animal rights. These include elected officials, national news anchors, professors, farmers, filmmakers, celebrities, and more. As a result of his dedication and passion for animal rights, Runkle was inducted into the US Animal Rights Hall of Fame in 2009. At age 25, he was the youngest inductee ever.

Nathan Runkle's Mercy for Animals organization staged an undercover investigation that swayed voters toward Proposition 2.

The MFA investigation illustrated the truth about conditions on the factory farms the activists visited. However, Proposition 2 supporters were up against a powerful foe: the agribusiness industry facing significant profit losses should Proposition 2 pass. In counterattacks, agribusiness labeled Proposition 2 supporters as extremists and the single largest threat to the US animal agriculture industry. The NO on Prop 2 campaign, which was in part funded by egg farmers, claimed the extraordinary expense for the proposed improvements would be passed on to consumers.

THE VOTES ARE IN

On November 4, 2008, voters in California went to the polls. At the end of the day, Proposition 2 passed by an overwhelming majority. It was described as "the single most important piece of legislation for farm animals in US history."[11] PETA characterized the victory as a positive step, but cautioned that only the basic needs of the animals would be met. They vowed to continue their efforts to eliminate the raising of animals for food.

The passage of Proposition 2 in California was historic. It addressed the abusive confinement conditions for animals on these farms. But the reality was that billions of animals across the country were still subject to cruelty on factory farms. In late 2011, MFA went undercover again at a Butterball turkey farm in North Carolina. MFA documented workers kicking, dragging, throwing, and stomping on turkeys. The workers received felony convictions for cruelty to animals in August 2012. It was the first such conviction related to birds used for food production in US history. However, although the workers were the ones prosecuted, MFA believed the Butterball company itself was responsible for creating a culture of cruelty.

Based on this belief, MFA went into another North Carolina Butterball farm in October 2012. They found that the abuse and neglect continued. Video footage revealed abuses almost identical to those found in 2011. Yet in December 2012, the prosecutor for the case declined to file animal cruelty charges.

BACKLASH

Even though agribusiness could not prevent the passage of Proposition 2, their counterattacks are far from over. After activists staged undercover

HUMANE SLAUGHTER ACT

The Humane Slaughter Act was passed in 1958, which required that animals be made insensible to pain prior to slaughter. In 1978 it was revised and renamed the Humane Methods of Slaughter Act. The new version allowed for government inspection of slaughterhouses to ensure proper handling and slaughter.

The law has serious flaws, however. First, it does not include birds. More than 9 billion chickens and turkeys are raised and killed each year in the United States.[12] And due to a flaw in the Humane Methods of Slaughter Act, they may still be conscious at the time of death. Also, slaughterhouses are not properly monitored. In one such case, a 2011 MFA undercover investigation revealed sadistic methods of slaughter of goats and sheep continuing at a California facility.

Finally, animal rights groups believe the act's ultimate flaw is that it still allows the slaughter of animals. They believe any slaughter is unconscionable, even if it is deemed "humane."

investigations during the factory farm campaign, agribusiness fought back. They succeeded in adopting what are known as "Ag Gag Laws" in five states in 2012. The laws essentially make the undercover investigations executed by PETA, MFA, and others illegal. They prohibit anyone from taking photos or video of animals on factory farms without permission. In early 2013, nine other states introduced legislation that would ban or restrict filming on farms.

History has shown that animal rights groups will not back down. Indeed, their fight to end factory farming continues today as does the fight to abolish altogether the raising of animals for food. Groups such as Mercy for Animals, PETA, Compassion Over Killing, and the Animal Legal Defense Fund all have ongoing anti–factory farming campaigns.

Animal rights groups realize that despite the progress »
they have seen, abuses still occur daily on factory farms.

CHAPTER 8

MOVING FORWARD

The animal rights movement has seen tremendous growth and progress since its roots in the antivivisectionist movement of the late 1800s and certainly since the 1970s. The number of animal rights groups has exploded. Membership in these groups increased into the millions by the early part of the new millennium.

The movement has seen many achievements. Countless laws protecting animals of all kinds exist at the federal level and in all 50 states. Alternatives to animal research are common practice today. Menu options at restaurants typically include vegetarian and vegan dishes because of the large increase in people choosing these lifestyles.

Without a doubt, the animal rights movement and ideology is increasingly a part of the public discussion. More people are thinking about how humans use animals and are taking action on their behalf. Yet despite all this, millions of animals are still exploited worldwide for food, clothing, entertainment, research, and more. Activists know there is much work yet to be done.

DEMOGRAPHICS THEN AND NOW

There have been many changes since Henry Bergh and Caroline Earle White began animal welfare reforms in the late 1800s. And yet, some aspects have not changed in more than a century. What has held true across the eras is the prominence of wealthy and educated members in these groups. Within the groups, women continue to make up the great majority of members—outnumbering their male counterparts four to one.[1] But despite the successes of the women's rights movement that ran concurrently to the animal rights movement, leadership within these organizations is still dominated by males.

CURRENT CAMPAIGNS

Factory farming is a still top priority for many animal rights activists. Yet there are other ongoing campaigns as well. These include antifur campaigns; the ongoing antivivisection movement; work to end hunting and trapping; fights to abolish horse and greyhound racing; campaigns to end the use of animals for work; and efforts to terminate bullfighting, cockfighting, dog fighting, and the like.

PETA continues work on a number of fronts. A current campaign aims to stop the use of live animals in military training exercises. PETA also has the Whose Skin Are You In? campaign to eliminate the use of animals for clothing materials, including leather, wool, and silk. In addition, the McCruelty campaign is ongoing. The campaign has a page on its Web site urging people to pledge to be cruelty free by purchasing only products not tested on animals. To help consumers, PETA and numerous other organizations list products on their Web sites to make cruelty-free shopping simpler.

Other animal rights activists are working to eliminate circuses that use animals as entertainment. Circus animals often experience abuse, deprivation, and confinement. The size of animals' enclosures is only minimally regulated by the federal government. In addition, circus animals are deprived of normal family and social groups. The living conditions thwart almost all natural animal behaviors.

A similar case can be made for zoos. Today, there is a zoo in almost every major city in the world. The original purpose of zoos was for mere public entertainment. In the 1970s, zoos' purpose shifted as people became attuned to the physical and emotional needs of wild animals. Animal habitats improved somewhat. Further, zoos began to justify their existence by arguing they provided public education and saved endangered species.

Animal rights activists, however, still work to abolish

"THE SADDEST SHOW ON EARTH"

The Ringling Bros. and Barnum & Bailey Circus is known as the "Greatest Show on Earth."[2] But animal rights activists firmly disagree. For example, activists cite that the circus's trainers "break" the elephants, which literally means breaking their spirits to make them dependent on trainers. Trainers do this by removing baby elephants from their mothers, using restraints, and beating elephants with bull hooks. These tactics cause enormous physical and psychological suffering for the animals. Officials for Ringling Bros. and Barnum & Bailey Circus deny these allegations.

PETA learned of these abuses and again went undercover in a multistate investigation. In 2009, they revealed trainers who beat elephants as a means to keep the animals in constant fear of punishment. Abuses also occur in the form of constant restraint in cramped boxcars without any mental or physical stimulation. PETA continues to stage protests outside the doors of ongoing Ringling Bros. and Barnum & Bailey Circus performances.

**LONELY,
SHACKLED,
ABUSED.**

BOYCOTT ZOOS.

PeTA

zoos. Activists assert that zoos do little to protect animals. Instead, they believe zoos simply teach people that caging animals and using them for entertainment is acceptable. Activists also stress that many zoo animals are in poor health and are neurotic. They advocate wildlife sanctuaries instead.

VEGANISM AND COMPASSIONATE LIVING

Another ongoing animal rights crusade is promoting veganism. According to a 2012 Gallup survey, 2 percent of Americans claim to be vegans.[3] For most people, becoming a vegan is more than just a dietary choice. It is a philosophy and lifestyle that promotes compassionate living beyond food. The Vegan Society, for example, defines a vegan as:

> *Someone who tries to live without exploiting animals, for the benefit of animals, people and the planet. Vegans eat a plant-based diet, with nothing coming from animals—no meat, milk, eggs or honey, for example. A vegan lifestyle also avoids leather, wool, silk and other animal products for clothing or any other purpose.*[4]

« **Dressed in costume, PETA activists stage a dramatic demonstration against zoos.**

CULTURAL CONDITIONING

Regardless of their ideological differences, animal rights activists all understand that in order to achieve ultimate goals, cultural conditioning and fundamental belief systems must change. To say the least, this is a major challenge. In US culture, people are raised to believe eating meat from a pig, chicken, cow, or fish is perfectly ethical, while the thought of eating a cat or dog is reprehensible. Psychologists understand these beliefs are so entrenched that people do not question petting and cuddling one animal while literally eating another. This belief system is known as *carnism*. It is the opposite of veganism.

Social psychologist Melanie Joy points out that cultural conditioning blocks people's awareness and thus the ability to make truly rational choices. Thus, culture enables people to engage in arguably inhumane practices, such as eating meat, without being fully aware of what they are doing. Likewise, such belief systems propagate the need for factory farms while also hiding the truth about what happens on those farms from public consciousness.

For many vegans, lifestyle goes beyond the exclusion of animal products from one's diet. It also means excluding the use of animals for clothing and all other purposes. In order to encourage more people to adopt this larger sense of a compassionate lifestyle, the Vegan Society and other organizations provide shopping guides, recipes, and information to ease the transition into veganism.

IDEOLOGY INTO THE FUTURE

The goal of the animal rights movement is the abolition of the exploitation of animals. Such a monumental goal inspires, yet confounds, the movement's activists and thinkers. Philosopher Tom Regan believes that in order to achieve the ultimate goals of the animal rights movement, the movement must grow astronomically. "I mean [by] billions and billions," he states.[5] In the face of this enormous challenge, Regan and others emphasize that animal rights activists must stay the course and work to change not only people's habits but also the fundamental belief systems in our world. He remarks, "Billions of people will embrace animal rights only if billions of people change in a deeper, more fundamental, a more revolutionary way."[6] To that end, he stresses,

> *What hope the animals have demands that we stay the course, for as long as we can—up to our last breath, in fact. That is the least we can do. And it is a very small pledge when compared to what animals are made to endure up to their last breath.*[7]

Legal scholar Gary Francione also subscribes to the abolitionist approach to animal rights. Like Regan, he is adamant that the movement's explicit goal must be the abolition of animal exploitation. He argues that although well intended, some rights groups achieve only welfare reforms. He argues reforms, such as those that merely improve conditions, are not enough. According to Francione, welfarist reform does nothing more than preserve and legitimize the entrenched exploitation of

Activists with an abolitionist ideology are not satisfied with reforms that merely improve conditions for exploited animals.

animals. For example, a ban on veal crates is not enough, as it does not end the exploitation of calves raised as food.

In order to truly achieve animal rights, he asserts groups must take action toward the "eradication of the property status of animals."[8] In this view, activists work step by step to end certain forms of exploitation on the path toward total abolition. For example, this approach seeks a complete ban on animal testing for products, not just a reduction in the number of animals used.

Within the animal rights movement, some activists adopt this abolitionist approach. Yet others see it as an all-or-nothing approach that is too unrealistic. They believe changing fundamental belief systems is an impossible task. Therefore, many animal rights activists adopt an incrementalist approach, choosing to work toward more achievable, pragmatic goals. Thus, even groups with the most genuine abolitionist aspirations deliberately design campaign strategies that will only improve conditions for animals. In this perspective, groups recognize that the elimination of veal crates does reduce some suffering for millions of calves. And while those activists realize it is not the end goal, they feel incremental victories such as this are steps toward a world where animals are treated with respect and compassion. As Alex Pacheco stated after the 1981 Silver Spring monkeys case,

> Difficult as it may be, I believe that tactfully and strategically we must combine parts of both approaches: we must fight for today's reforms while aiming for and advocating total abolition.[9]

Regardless of their ideologies and approaches, all animal rights activists play their roles in the movement to create a more compassionate society. They work on many different fronts, in many different ways, in the hope that

one day animals will be free from human exploitation.
As Runkle explained,

> *There is a special place for each person within*
> *the animal advocacy movement. I'm a strong*
> *believer that no matter who you are, where you're*
> *from, how old you are, or what your background*
> *is, you can take your own special and unique*
> *skills and talents and put them to use making*
> *the world a kinder place for animals.*[10] ●

Activists continue working toward a day when »
animals are no longer used for food, clothing,
entertainment, or experimentation.

TIMELINE

1789 British philosopher Jeremy Bentham argues animals are sentient beings worthy of moral consideration.

1809 The Liverpool Society for Preventing Wanton Cruelty to Brute Animals is founded on October 25.

1822 Martin's Act is passed in Great Britain.

1866 Henry Bergh establishes the American Society for the Prevention of Cruelty to Animals on April 10.

1883 Caroline Earle White establishes the American Anti-Vivisection Society.

1958 The Humane Slaughter Act is passed.

1975 Peter Singer publishes *Animal Liberation*.

1975 Henry Spira launches a publicity campaign against the American Museum of Natural History in New York.

1979 In an effort to end the Draize test, Spira begins an ad campaign against Revlon.

1980 Ingrid Newkirk and Alex Pacheco found People for the Ethical Treatment of Animals.

1981 The Farm Animal Reform Movement is established in July; on September 11, police raid the Institute for Behavioral Research.

1983 Tom Regan publishes *The Case for Animal Rights*.

1990 On June 10, the March for the Animals is held in Washington, DC.

1993 The NIH Revitalization Act is passed, ordering the NIH to implement the three *R*s: replacement, reduction, and refinement.

2002 Florida voters support the elimination of gestation crates.

2008 On November 4, California voters pass Proposition 2.

2012 Five states adopt "Ag Gag Laws" to prevent undercover investigations on factory farms.

PUBLIC OPINION ON MEDICAL TESTING ON ANIMALS

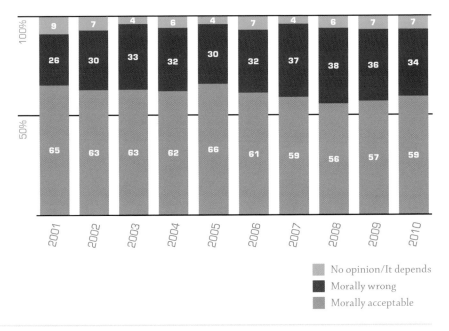

Year	No opinion/It depends	Morally wrong	Morally acceptable
2001	9	26	65
2002	7	30	63
2003	4	33	63
2004	6	32	62
2005	4	30	66
2006	7	32	61
2007	4	37	59
2008	6	38	56
2009	7	36	57
2010	7	34	59

No opinion/It depends
Morally wrong
Morally acceptable

DATE OF THE MOVEMENT'S BEGINNING

The animal welfare movement had roots in the 1860s; the modern animal rights movement took shape in the 1970s.

LOCATIONS

Great Britain; the United States; worldwide

KEY PLAYERS

Peter Singer wrote *Animal Liberation*, the movement's most important founding book.

US VEGETARIANS AND VEGANS

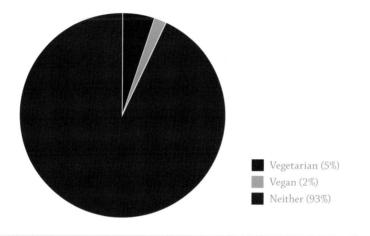

- Vegetarian (5%)
- Vegan (2%)
- Neither (93%)

Henry Spira helped push the movement from philosophical discussions into action.

Ingrid Newkirk and **Alex Pacheco** founded People for the Ethical Treatment of Animals.

GOALS AND OUTCOMES

The first groups formed in the mid-1800s to protect animals' welfare. By the 1970s, the movement took off with people arguing animals have equal rights to humans and should not be exploited for human use. The movement's ultimate goal is full liberation for animals; incremental goals include increasing veganism, ending factory farming, and stopping animal experiments.

GLOSSARY

activist
Someone who protests or speaks out against a social, political, economic, or moral wrong.

advocate
One who supports and speaks on behalf of another.

agribusiness
The industry associated with large-scale farming.

coalition
A temporary alliance of differing individuals or groups to achieve a common goal.

ethics
A theory or system of moral values.

euthanize
To purposely kill an animal in a relatively painless way.

exploit
To use something or someone unfairly for one's own advantage.

humane
Showing kindness and compassion.

ideology
The ideas and theories of an individual or group.

livestock
Farm animals raised for specific uses, such as to be food.

lobby
To attempt to change a politician's position on an issue.

neurotic

Being emotionally or mentally unstable.

pragmatic

Practical, as compared to idealistic.

sanctuary

A place of protection; a refuge.

sentient

Responsive, conscious, or thinking.

utilitarians

Believers in the philosophy that animals can be used for human purposes but suffering should be minimized.

ADDITIONAL RESOURCES

SELECTED BIBLIOGRAPHY

Beers, Diane L. *For the Prevention of Cruelty: The History and Legacy of Animal Rights Activism in the United States*. Athens, Ohio: Swallow Press/Ohio UP, 2006. Print.

Finsen, Lawrence and Susan Finsen. *The Animal Rights Movement in America: From Compassion to Respect*. New York: Twayne/Macmillan, 1994. Print.

Francione, Gary L. *Rain without Thunder: The Ideology of the Animal Rights Movement*. Philadelphia: Temple UP, 1996. Print.

Silverstein, Helena. *Unleashing Rights: Law, Meaning and the Animal Rights Movement*. Ann Arbor: U of Michigan P, 1996. Print.

Waldau, Paul. *Animal Rights: What Everyone Needs to Know*. New York: Oxford UP, 2011. Print.

FURTHER READINGS

Baur, Gene. *Farm Sanctuary: Changing Hearts and Minds about Animals and Food*. New York: Touchstone, 2008. Print.

Bekoff, Marc. *Animals Matter: A Biologist Explains Why We Should Treat Animals with Compassion and Respect*. Boston: Shambhala, 2008. Print.

Joy, Melanie. *Why We Love Dogs, Eat Pigs and Wear Cows: An Introduction to Carnism*. Canari: San Francisco, 2010. Print.

Lyman, Howard F. *No More Bull!: The Mad Cowboy Targets America's Worst Enemy: Our Diet*. New York: Scribner, 2005. Print.

WEB SITES

To learn more about the animal rights movement, visit ABDO Publishing Company online at **www.abdopublishing.com**. Web sites about the animal rights movement are featured on our Book Links page. These links are routinely monitored and updated to provide the most current information available.

PLACES TO VISIT

Animal Rights National Conference

888-327-6872
http://www.arconference.org
Attend "the world's largest and longest-running animal rights gathering." The event includes numerous speakers, workshops, exhibits, videos, and more. See the event Web site for annual conference location and information.

Vegetarian Summerfest

518-568-7970
http://www.vegetariansummerfest.org
Attend the annual conference to learn more about a vegetarian lifestyle! Learn about vegetarian health, nutrition, and diet, and experience meals cooked by a professional chef. See the event Web site for annual conference location and information.

SOURCE NOTES

CHAPTER 1. SILVER SPRING MONKEYS

1. "Silver Spring Monkeys: Video." *PETA*. PETA, n.d. Web. 20 May 2013.

2. Deborah Blum. *Monkey Wars*. New York: Oxford UP, 1994. Print. 107.

3. "Silver Spring Monkeys: Video." *PETA*. PETA, n.d. Web. 20 May 2013.

4. Peter Singer, ed. "The Silver Spring Monkeys." *In Defense of Animals*. New York: Basil Blackwell, 1985. Print. 138.

5. Ian Redmond. *The Primate Family Tree*. Buffalo, NY: Firefly, 2008. Print. 29.

6. Stefan Lovgren. "Chimps, Humans 96 Percent the Same, Gene Study Finds." *National Geographic News*. National Geographic Society, 31 Aug. 2005. Web. 20 May 2013.

7. Brian M. Lowe. *Emerging Moral Vocabularies: The Creation and Establishment of New Forms of Moral And Ethical Meanings*. Lanham, MD: Lexington, 2006. Print. 184.

CHAPTER 2. ROOTS OF THE MOVEMENT

1. Jeremy Bentham. "An Introduction to the Principles of Morals and Legislation." *Library of Economics and Liberty*. Liberty Fund, 2002. Web. 20 May 2013.

2. Ella Wheeler Wilcox. "The Voice of the Voiceless." *Ella Wheeler Wilcox*. Richard A. Edwards, 5 Nov. 2011. Web. 20 May 2013.

3. Diane L. Beers. *For the Prevention of Cruelty: The History and Legacy of Animal Rights Activism in the United States*. Athens, OH: Swallow Press/Ohio UP, 2006. Print. 26.

CHAPTER 3. NEW VISIONS

1. Diane L. Beers. *For the Prevention of Cruelty: The History and Legacy of Animal Rights Activism in the United States*. Athens, OH: Swallow Press/Ohio UP, 2006. Print. 128–130.

2. Helena Silverstein. *Unleashing Rights. Law, Meaning and the Animal Rights Movement*. Ann Arbor: University of Michigan, 1996. Print. 43.

3. "History." *The Vegan Society*. The Vegan Society, n.d. Web. 20 May 2013.

4. Ibid.

CHAPTER 4. IDEOLOGY INTO ACTION

1. "Animal People: The Humane Movement in America, Part 1 of 3." *Vimeo*. United Action for Animals, 2011. Web. 20 May 2013.

2. Ibid.

3. Ibid.

4. Singer, Peter. *Animal Liberation: The Definitive Classic of the Animal Movement*. New York: HarperCollins, 2009. Print. 6.

5. Ibid.

6. Lawrence and Susan Finsen. *The Animal Rights Movement in America: From Compassion to Respect*. New York: Twayne/Macmillan, 1994. Print. 3.

7. Peter Singer. "RE: Questions for a Book." Message to the author. 19 Dec. 2012. E-mail.

8. David Zax. "A Brief History of House Cats." *Smithsonian.com*, Smithsonian Institution, 1 July 2007. Web. 20 May 2013.

9. Peter Singer. *Ethics Into Action: Henry Spira and the Animal Rights Movement*. Lanham, MD: Rowman & Littlefield, 1998. Print. 93.

10. "Henry Spira: Animal Rights Activist." *You Tube*. You Tube, 12 Feb. 2010. Web. 20 May 2013.

11. Peter Singer, ed. *In Defense of Animals*. New York: Basil Blackwell, 1985. Print. 205–206.

12. Stephanie Ostfeld. "The Lives of Three Extraordinary Individuals." *AV Magazine*. American Anti-Vivisection Society, Fall 2000. Web. 20 May 2013.

13. Michael Allen Fox. "History Lesson: Looking at the Animal Rights Movement over Time." *AV Magazine*. American Anti-Vivisection Society, Fall 2000. Web. 20 May 2013.

14. "About NAVS." *NAVS*. North American Vegetarian Society, n.d. Web. 20 May 2013.

CHAPTER 5. THE MOVEMENT TAKES OFF

1. Deborah Blum. *Monkey Wars*. New York: Oxford UP, 1994. Print. 107.

2. Lawrence and Susan Finsen. *The Animal Rights Movement in America: From Compassion to Respect*. New York: Twayne/Macmillan, 1994. Print. 77.

3. "About PETA." *PETA*. PETA, n.d. Web. 20 May 2013.

4. Ibid.

5. Lawrence and Susan Finsen. *The Animal Rights Movement in America: From Compassion to Respect*. New York: Twayne/Macmillan, 1994. Print. 67–71.

6. "FARM's Approach." *FARM*. Farm Animal Rights Movement, n.d. Web. 20 May 2013.

7. "About Meatout." *Meatout*. Farm Animal Rights Movement, n.d. Web. 20 May 2013.

8. Lawrence and Susan Finsen. *The Animal Rights Movement in America: From Compassion to Respect*. New York: Twayne/Macmillan, 1994. Print. 7–9.

9. "What Is Past Is Prologue." *Tom Regan's Rights & Writes*. The Animals Voice, 2012. Web. 20 May 2013.

10. "Animal People: The Humane Movement in America, Part 3 of 3." *Vimeo*. United Action for Animals, 2011. Web. 20 May 2013.

CHAPTER 6. GAINING MOMENTUM

1. Lawrence and Susan Finsen. *The Animal Rights Movement in America: From Compassion to Respect*. New York: Twayne/Macmillan, 1994. Print. 72.

2. "Integrating Animal Interests into Our Legal System." *LexisNexis*. LexisNexis, 2004. Web. 20 May 2013.

3. "Animal Rights Activists March on Washington." *Victoria Advocate*. Google News, 11 June 1990. Web. 20 May 2013.

4. "Famous Join Rally for Rights Animal Testing Protested in DC." *SunSentinel.com*, SunSentinel, 11 June 1990. Web. 20 May 2013.

5. Michael Ollove. "Animal Rights Group Stages a GM Bash." *Baltimore Sun*. Tribune Newspaper, 20 Jan. 1992. Web. 20 May 2013.

6. Lisa Yount. *Animal Rights*. New York: Facts on File, 2008. Print. 53.

7. Ibid.

8. "Lab Animal Welfare." *MSPCA–Angell*. MSPCA–Angell, 2013. Web. 20 May 2013.

9. "Alternatives to Animal Testing." *PETA*. PETA, n.d. Web. 20 May 2013.

10. "10 Questions for Ingrid Newkirk." *Time Video*. Time, n.d. Web. 20 May 2013.

CHAPTER 7. FOCUS ON FARMING

1. Beth Krause. "Being Grateful for the Meat We Eat." *The Whole Story*. Whole Foods Market, Inc., 20 Jan. 2013. 20 May 2013.

2. "Animal People: The Humane Movement in America, Part 2 of 3." *Vimeo*. United Action for Animals, 2011. Web. 20 May 2013.

3. Patricia Haddock. "Rights vs. Welfare, Updated Timeline, Key Orgs." Message to the author. 5 Dec. 2012. E-mail.

4. "Florida's Historic Ban on Gestation Crates." *Animal Rights Foundation of Florida*. Animal Rights Foundation of Florida, n.d. Web. 20 May 2013.

5. "About Us." *Farm Sanctuary*. Farm Sanctuary, n.d. Web. 20 May 2013.

6. "The History of McDonald's Cruelty." *McCruelty.com*. PETA, n.d. Web. 20 May 2013.

7. Ibid.

8. "National Conference to End Factory Farming: Paul Shapiro." *You Tube*. You Tube, October 2011. Web. 20 May 2013.

9. "Under Cover at a California Factory Egg Farm." *Mercy for Animals*. Mercy for Animals, n.d. Web. 20 May 2013.

10. Dan Noyes. "New Ammunition for Prop 2 Supporters." *ABC 7 News*. ABC Inc., 13 Oct. 2008. Web. 20 May 2013.

11. "Californians Deliver Decisive Victory to Prevent Factory Farm Cruelty by Passing Prop 2." *Humane Society of the United States*. Humane Society of the United States, 5 Nov. 2008. Web. 20 May 2013.

12. L. Murray. "Factory-Farmed Chickens: Their Difficult Lives and Deaths." *Encyclopedia Britannica Advocacy for Animals*. Encyclopedia Britannica, 14 May 2007. Web. 20 May 2013.

CHAPTER 8. MOVING FORWARD

1. Lyle Munro. *Compassionate Beasts: The Quest for Animal Rights*. Westport, CT: Praeger, 2001. Print. 61.

2. "Ringling Bros. and Barnum & Bailey." *Ringling Bros. and Barnum & Bailey*. Feld Entertainment, 2013. Web. 20 May 2013.

3. Frank Newport. "In U.S., 5% Consider Themselves Vegetarians." *GALLUP Wellbeing*. Gallup, Inc., 26 July 2012. Web. 20 May 2013.

4. "Why Vegan?" *The Vegan Society*. The Vegan Society, n.d. Web. 20 May 2013.

5. Tom Regan. "Vegan Choice." *Tom Regan's Animal Rights & Writes*. Tom Regan's Animal Rights & Writes, n.d. Web. 20 May 2013.

6. Ibid.

7. Ibid.

8. Gary L. Francione. *Rain Without Thunder: The Ideology of the Animal Rights Movement*. Philadelphia: Temple UP, 1996. Print. 1–6.

9. Peter Singer, ed. *In Defense of Animals*. New York: Basil Blackwell, 1985. Print. 147.

10. Gary Smith. "Interview with Nathan Runkle, Founder & Executive Director of Mercy For Animals." *Elephant Journal*. Waylon H. Lewis Enterprises, 2 June 2010. Web. 20 May 2013.

INDEX

ABOUT THE AUTHOR

Laura Perdew is a middle school teacher and author. She writes fiction and nonfiction for children of all ages and has also published *Kids on the Move! Colorado*, a guide for parents traveling through Colorado with small children. She lives in Boulder, Colorado, with her husband and twin boys.

ABOUT THE CONSULTANT

Joe Gaziano is a professor in the Political Science Department at Lewis University, where he teaches undergraduate classes in American government. Joe is an animal activist who has worked for SPEAK, a national humane education organization. He has given speeches on animal rights, vegetarianism, and factory farming to students in elementary schools, high schools, and college. He has also spoken at several animal rights conferences. Joe was also a regular contributor to *Good Karma* magazine, a SPEAK publication in the Chicago area.